WILD ABOUT
FUDGE

BY MARILYN MYERLY

BARRON'S

New York • London • Toronto • Sydney

To my mother Rodna Hughes—the best cook

All inquiries should be addressed to:
Barron's Educational Series, Inc.
250 Wireless Boulevard
Hauppauge, NY 11788

International Standard Book No. 0-8120-4161-5

Library of Congress Card Catalog No. 89-6710

Library of Congress Cataloging-in-Publication Data

Myerly, Marilyn.
  Wild about fudge / by Marilyn Myerly.
      p. cm.
  Includes index.
  ISBN 0-8120-4161-5
  1. Fudge. I. Title.
TX791.M94   1989
641.6'374—dc20   89-6710
                                      CIP

Design by Milton Glaser, Inc.
Color photographs by Matthew Klein
Julie Gong, prop stylist
Ann Disrude, home economist

PRINTED IN HONG KONG

901   4900   987654321

CONTENTS

INTRODUCTION

If I were to tell you I can still remember the first batch of perfect fudge I made 25 years ago, how rich and smooth it was; how the sugar melted in, leaving no grainy crystals, you might get an idea of how much I like fudge.

But then, if I were to describe how I packed a suitcase full of pots and headed to the Grand Canyon National Park (about 7,000 feet above sea level) to learn how to cook fudge at high altitudes, you'd have to conclude that I'm wild about fudge.

I am.

And ever since my success 25 years ago, I've been on a quest to duplicate it. At first I resigned myself to satisfying my cravings at Mrs. See's Candy Store.

Then, a few years ago my passion took hold. I went to the library and read everything I could about candy making. I went through more pounds of sugar than all the students in the local high school combined; I single-handedly caused a run on cocoa at my grocery store. Finally, after five months of experiments I was able to make perfect fudge, consistently.

I'm sharing my secrets for pure, delicious fool-proof fudge: fudge that has a full flavor and smooth texture and is able to hold deep, soft, swirling folds, just as it does in my fudge fantasies.

My method for perfect fudge requires cooking the candy within a certain time period to a specific temperature, and then stirring until the thick, glossy mass holds its shape. These fudges are made with pure ingredients, not fillers like marshmallow creme, which are common. Each step is carefully described. Timing the cooking takes the guesswork out of the whole process, and you'll be rewarded with a plate of fudge in only 30 minutes.

It's a far cry from the recipes Vassar and Wellesley women were making late at night in their dormitories in the late 1800s. Their slapdash technique—cooking the candy over alcohol lamps—might have led them to use the popular expletive of the time: "Oh, fudge!"

I'm gratified that fudge making has become so much easier since those rudimentary experiments. Instead of expletives, I'm hearing praise from cooks who are making batch after marvelous batch of candy.

The wonderful recipes that follow assure you of a variety of fudge tastes, from the traditional chocolate to new tropical flavors.

There are fudges you'll love to give as gifts, as well as those you'll want to horde in the back of the cupboard. I'm sure you too will be Wild About Fudge.

CONVERSION TABLES

The weights and measures in the lists of ingredients and cooking instructions for each recipe are in both U.S. and metric units.

LIQUID MEASURES

The Imperial cup is considerably larger than the U. S. cup. Use the following table to convert to Imperial liquid units.

AMERICAN CUP (in book)	IMPERIAL CUP (adjusts to)
¼ cup	4 tablespoons
½ cup	8 tablespoons
1 cup	¼ pint + 6 tablespoons

Note: The Australian and Canadian cup measures 250 mL and is only slightly larger than the U. S. cup, which is 236mL. Cooks in Australia and Canada can follow the exact measurements given in the recipes, using either the U. S. or metric measures.

SOLID MEASURES

British and Australian cooks measure more items by weight. Here are approximate equivalents for basic items in the book.

	U. S. Customary	Imperial
Butter	3 tablespoons	1½ oz.
	2 tablespoons	1 oz.

	U. S. Customary	Imperial
Chocolate, unsweetened baking	2½ oz.	2½ oz.
Cocoa	½ cup	1½ oz.
	¼ cup	¾ oz.
Coconut, dried	¼ cup	1 oz.
Fruit, dried	¼ cup	1 oz.
Nuts	½ cup	2 oz.
Peanut or other nut butters	¼ cup	2½ oz.
Sugar, granulated	2 cups	16 oz.
Sugar, light brown	2¼ cups, packed	16 oz.

Note: Accurate measurements of syrups and extract flavorings are very important when making fudge. The American tablespoon holds 15 mL and the teaspoon 5 mL. British tablespoons tend to be larger. Use a scant British tablespoon to each American tablespoon.

A NOTE ABOUT INGREDIENTS

The names for ingredients used in this book are terms that will be familiar to U.S. and Canadian cooks. For cooks in England and Australia, be aware of the following:

> *Baking soda = bicarbonate of soda*
> *Canned evaporated milk = unsweetened whole milk with about 60% of the water removed.*
> *Heavy or whipping cream = double cream*
> *Light corn syrup = golden cane syrup*
> *Sugar = granulated white sugar*
> *Unsulphured molasses = a light molasses*
> *Unsweetened baking chocolate = bitter, baker's, baking or cooking chocolate.*

Opposite: Tools and ingredients

ABOUT THE INGREDIENTS

For your convenience you may make substitutions of some ingredients.

BUTTER

Preferable because of its superior flavor but margarine may be substituted. Salted butter is used in all recipes. Unsalted may be used.

CHOCOLATE

For true flavor, we use only pure chocolate but you have your choice of three different kinds. It's fun to make fudge with all three and have a taste comparison test with chocolate-loving friends.

UNSWEETENED BAKING CHOCOLATE

This is chocolate liquor processed from cocoa beans and molded into the familiar packaged blocks or squares. Fudge made with this chocolate has a slight grain.

REGULAR, NATURAL OR AMERICAN COCOA SUCH AS HERSHEY'S

The same chocolate liquor with some of the cocoa butter, which has no chocolate flavor, removed. This chocolate is then pulverized to a fine powder known everywhere as 100% pure cocoa. Fudge made with cocoa has the smoothest texture. To measure, spoon cocoa lightly into measuring cup, then level.

Opposite: Cooking phase

DUTCH PROCESS COCOA

Cocoa treated with a mild alkali, which neutralizes the natural acids in the cocoa. This "softens" the cocoa, making it less bitter. For years I thought its darker color meant it was stronger. It's not, but the flavor is decidedly different. Various brands differ in taste, too.

EXTRACT FLAVORINGS

Use the very best. Select pure extracts whenever possible; always use pure, not imitation, vanilla. Schilling/McCormick and Wagner's are excellent. For information on the availability of these extracts contact:

> *McCormick and Company, Inc.*
> *211 Schilling Circle*
> *Hunt Valley, MD 21031*
> *Tel. 1(800) 632-5847*

> *John Wagner and Sons, Inc.*
> *900 Jacksonville Road*
> *Ivyland, PA 18974*
> *Tel. (215) 674-5000*

If a fine extract is not available, make a fudge flavored primarily with chocolate, coffee, peanut butter, caramel, honey, brown sugar or molasses. These flavors are pure and available everywhere.

FRUIT, DRIED

Enrich fudges with any kind of dried non-sugared fruit—raisins, apricots, sour cherries or peaches, or whatever appeals to you. Unusual dried fruits may be found in gourmet or health food stores. If you have dried fruit coated with sugar or if you choose to use packaged dried coconut (it's dusted with fine sugar), wash the sugar crystals away and press the fruit very dry between the folds of a clean towel. If preparing fresh coconut, grate, then roast the shreds in a 350°F oven until completely dry.

CITRUS RIND

Grate only the colored part of the rind.

LIQUOR, LIQUEURS

For an interesting change, try adding ¼ cup liquor or liqueur to the recipes. Even vodka will make a difference. The non-chocolate creme fudges in particular are flavored subtly and deliciously by these beverages. Since the alcohol is cooked off, only the flavor remains. Do not add alcohol to fudges containing brown sugar or Dutch process cocoa. The texture will be poor.

MILK AND CREAM

Heavy cream, half and half, or a mixture of ¾ cup (180 mL) canned evaporated milk and ¼ cup (60 mL) water may be substituted for milk in any of the recipes.

NUTS

Usually best left whole. Stir unsalted nuts into fudge. To remove salt from nuts, rinse in water and press dry between the folds of a clean towel. For really nutty fudge, add a full cup and then some.

TO ROAST NUTS

Spread nuts out on a cookie sheet and roast in a 350°F oven until the nuts turn a light brown. Watch closely and stir frequently. You may also roast nuts in a heavy skillet on the stove top using ½ teaspoon cooking oil for each ½ cup (60 g) nuts. Use medium heat and stir constantly.

SYRUPS

Scrape measuring spoon to ensure full measure.

EQUIPMENT

COOKING PAN

Heavy 4-quart pan measuring about 7 or 8 inches across the bottom. This allows the thermometer to be properly submerged.

STIRRING PAN

Cake pan type, approximately 9 × 13 inches and at least ½ inch deep.

STIRRING SPOON

Wooden spoons are ideal, and a paddle shape moves more syrup across the bottom of the pan. This helps prevent burning.

MEASURING CUPS AND SPOONS

Use standard sizes and level measurements.

METAL SPATULA

Pancake-turner type

WRAPPING PAPER

Plastic wrap or bags seal efficiently.

CANDY THERMOMETER

The larger the better for easy reading. A thermometer measuring at least 5 inches between the 100°F and 400°F markings works well.

HOW TO MAKE PERFECT FUDGE

Perfect fudge results when the ingredients are cooked to a final, or finish, temperature within a certain time period. Fudge cooked this way is creamy smooth and capable of holding itself in soft, beautiful folds.

Finish cooking temperatures vary for everyone depending on where you live, the candy thermometer you use and, occasionally, the ingredients in the recipe.

Follow these simple steps to find your finish temperature.

- *Place thermometer in a small pan with 3 inches of water and the bulb ½ inch above bottom of pan. Let water boil briskly for 4 minutes.*

- *Without removing thermometer from the boiling water, and having your eyes at the same level as the top of the mercury column, read the thermometer carefully in either "F" (Fahrenheit) or "C" (Celsius) degrees. Jot down the reading. This is your FIRST temperature level and it is the basis for figuring the FINISH temperature of your fudge. Success depends on the accuracy of this reading.*

- *Add 10°F (5°C) to that number. This is your second temperature level.*

- *Add 6°F (4°C) more. This is your third temperature level.*

- *Add 10°F (5°C) more. This is your final or finish temperature level.**

These temperature levels will help you to time the cooking of the fudge. The goal is for the fudge to cook for 15 minutes between the first and finish temperature levels. You have a few minutes' leeway either way.

Set thermometer in a dry spot to cool

Whenever you use a new thermometer or cooking a different location, check your finish temperature again.

---

*Do not add 10°F, 6°F and 10°F to Easy Chocolate Fudge, Caramel Creme Fudge, or Pure Maple Creme Fudge.

GOOD TO KNOW

- *One batch of fudge takes about 30 minutes to prepare.*

- *Do not double or halve the recipes.*

- *The more extract in fudge, the longer the stirring time.*

- *Read thermometer at eye level in the pan. To remove it and read it will result in fudge failure.*

- *Do not put a cool thermometer into hot liquid.*

- *Set a hot thermometer in a dry spot to cool. A clean large coffee cup is a good container.*

- *To clean the thermometer, soak in a large cup of warm water. The sticky syrup will dissolve.*

- *Let the children clean the pans. They'll love it.*

- *The Ultimate Pure Chocolate Fudge recipe has all the chocolate it can hold. Try it with half the chocolate; some say a lighter taste is even more flavorful.*

- *Fudge cooked 3°F to 4°F too high or low may fail. Read thermometer carefully.*

Opposite: Pouring fudge into stirring pan

COOKING ON AN ELECTRIC STOVE OR BURNER

Once you find the setting where fudge will cook for about 15 minutes between the first and finish temperature levels, it will not be necessary to adjust the heat during cooking.

TIMING THE COOKING

When sugar is cooked with syrup, the syrup causes the sugar to invert or become syrupy, too. The longer the mixture cooks, the more sugar inverts, so that long cooking or too much syrup will result in syrupy fudge. Syrups, properly used, give fudge a silky, smooth texture.

STIRRING FUDGE IN THE COOKING PAN

Contrary to popular belief, you can stir fudge as it cooks and scrape the sugared syrup on the sides of the pan back into the fudge. Frequent stirring prevents burning.

STIRRING FUDGE IN THE STIRRING PAN

As the fudge cools in the stirring pan, sugar crystals begin to form. Stirring will result in a creamy, smooth textured fudge.

COOKING ON A RAINY DAY

Go right ahead. These candies are cooked to the highest possible temperature for fudge, so they are not adversely affected by high humidity.

COOKING AT DIFFERENT ALTITUDES

Due to the pressure of air upon the earth, water boils at 212°F (100°C) at sea level and 1°F lower for each 500 feet in elevation. Regardless of

Opposite: Adding butter, extract, and nuts

how long water boils or how hot the flame, it will never rise above these figures. (This is true of water only. When other ingredients are heated to boiling, the temperature continues to rise.)

Fudge must cook to a certain specific number of degrees (usually 26°F) above the boiling point of water to allow the right amount of evaporation of the candy syrup. Since the boiling point varies at different altitudes, finish temperatures will differ.

CHOCOLATE FUDGES

THE ULTIMATE PURE CHOCOLATE FUDGE

MAKES 1 POUND

INGREDIENTS

2 cups (450 g) sugar
1 cup (240 mL) milk
½ cup (45 g) cocoa (regular type
such as Hershey's)
or 2½ ounces (70 g)
unsweetened baking chocolate
3 tablespoons light corn syrup
¼ teaspoon salt
3 tablespoons (42 g) butter
Optional: ¾ teaspoon instant
coffee granules
2 tablespoons (28 g) butter, cut
into several pieces
1 teaspoon vanilla extract
Optional: ½ cup (60 g) nuts
and/or dried fruit

Find your finish temperature on page 14.

Set out on countertop stirring pan, 20-inch sheet of plastic wrap, spatula, timer or clock, and paper and pencil.

Combine sugar, milk, cocoa or chocolate, corn syrup, salt, 3 tablespoons butter and coffee in cooking pan. Place thermometer in pan with bulb ½ inch off the bottom. Leave in place until fudge is done. Turn heat to medium high. On a gas stove, look at flame at eye level. Turn flame to highest point, then back to medium; carefully adjust to medium high. On a large electric burner, medium heat may be appropriate. Stir to mix well.

When your first temperature level is reached, set a timer for 5 minutes (or jot down the time and watch a clock). Stir frequently or constantly if your pan is thin. Scrape sides and bottom of pan as you stir. After 5 minutes, thermometer should reach your second temperature level. If it reads higher, slightly lower heat. If it reads lower, slightly raise heat.

Immediately set timer for 5 minutes again. After this 5 minutes, the thermometer should reach your third temperature level. If it reads higher or lower, adjust heat as before.

Stir constantly now and watch thermometer closely. In about 5 minutes, when thermometer reaches your EXACT finish temperature, IM-MEDIATELY REMOVE FROM HEAT. Remove thermometer.

POUR INTO STIRRING PAN: Do not scrape cooking pan. Let fudge cool at room temperature for 5 minutes. Add remaining butter, vanilla extract and nuts or fruit.

BEGIN STIRRING: Use a clean sturdy spoon. Stir in an easy, steady manner. Do not beat or use an electric mixer. Scrape sides and all parts of pan. Fudge thickens and holds its own shape in 4 to 10 minutes. TO KNOW IF FUDGE

HAS THICKENED ENOUGH: Stop stirring. Count off 5 seconds. If fudge is still spreading out, resume stirring. Repeat until fudge holds its shape. WITHOUT A MOMENT'S DELAY, SCOOP FUDGE ONTO PLASTIC WRAP, USING THE SPATULA. Cool. Wrap tightly. Fudge tastes best after it has aged for 12 hours.

Variations

CHOCOLATE BURNT ALMOND FUDGE
Roast the almonds until some look slightly burned.

Use half the cocoa or unsweetened chocolate. Add ½ teaspoon almond extract and ¾ cup (90 g) roasted, slivered almonds to the stirring pan. Omit coffee.

CHOCOLATE BANANA FUDGE
Use half the cocoa or unsweetened chocolate. Substitute 1½ teaspoons banana extract for vanilla. Omit coffee.

CHOCOLATE CHERRY FUDGE

Use half the cocoa or unsweetened chocolate. Substitute 2 teaspoons cherry extract for vanilla. Omit coffee.

Optional: ½ cup (60 g) nuts and/or ½ cup (60 g) minced, dried pitted sour cherries.

CHOCOLATE COCONUT PECAN FUDGE

Use half the cocoa or unsweetened chocolate. Substitute 1 teaspoon coconut extract for vanilla. Add ¼ cup (30 g) pecans and ¼ cup (30 g) dried coconut. Omit coffee.

CHOCOLATE HONEY FUDGE

Use regular cocoa. Reduce sugar to 1¾ cups (400 g). Substitute 2 tablespoons honey for the corn syrup. Add ⅛ teaspoon baking soda to the cooking pan.* Omit salt and coffee.

---

*Baking soda and alcohol may cause the cooking syrup to foam to the top of the pan. Lower heat until foaming subsides.

CHOCOLATE KAHLÚA FUDGE

Add ¼ cup (60 mL) Kahlúa liqueur* and ¾ teaspoon instant coffee granules to the cooking pan.

CHOCOLATE ORANGE FUDGE

Substitute 1 teaspoon orange extract for vanilla. Add 1 tablespoon grated orange rind to the stirring pan.

CHOCOLATE MINT FUDGE

Substitute ½ teaspoon peppermint extract for vanilla. Omit coffee.

CHOCOLATE MOLASSES FUDGE

Substitute 2 tablespoons unsulphured molasses for corn syrup. Add ¼ teaspoon baking soda to the cooking pan.* Omit coffee.

CHOCOLATE PEANUT BUTTER FUDGE

For extra flavor, knead into an attractive shape and press salted peanuts on top. Use half the cocoa or unsweetened chocolate. Add ¼ cup (65 g) crunchy or smooth peanut butter to the stirring pan. Omit coffee.

Optional: ½ cup (60 g) peanuts.

CHOCOLATE RUM FUDGE
The rum strengthens the chocolate. Add ¼ cup (60 mL) rum,* dark preferred, to the cooking pan. Omit coffee.

CHOCOLATE FUDGE SUPREME
Substitute 1 cup (240 mL) heavy cream for the milk.

---

*Alcohol may cause the cooking syrup to foam to the top of the pan. Lower heat until foaming subsides.

CHOCOLATE BLACK WALNUT FUDGE

MAKES 1 POUND

INGREDIENTS

2 cups (450 g) sugar
1 cup (240 mL) milk
½ cup (45 g) cocoa (regular type
such as Hershey's)
or 2½ ounces (75 g)
unsweetened baking chocolate
3 tablespoons light corn syrup
¼ teaspoon salt
3 tablespoons (42 g) butter
Optional: ¾ teaspoon instant
coffee granules
2 tablespoons (28 g) butter, cut
into several pieces
1 teaspoon vanilla extract
½ cup (60 g) black walnuts

Black walnut fudge is special; perhaps no other nut flavors so distinctly.

Find your finish temperature on page 14.

Set out on countertop stirring pan, 20-inch sheet of plastic wrap, spatula, timer or clock, and paper and pencil.

Combine sugar, milk, cocoa or chocolate, corn syrup, salt, 3 tablespoons butter and coffee in cooking pan. Place thermometer in pan with bulb ½ inch off the bottom. Leave in place until fudge is done. Turn heat to medium high. On a gas stove, look at flame at eye level. Turn flame to highest point, then back to medium; carefully adjust to medium high. On a large electric burner, medium heat may be appropriate. Stir to mix well.

When your first temperature level is reached, set a timer for 5 minutes (or jot down the time and watch a clock). Stir frequently or constantly if your pan is thin. Scrape sides and bottom

Opposite: Scooping fudge onto plastic wrap

of pan as you stir. After 5 minutes, thermometer should reach your second temperature level. If it reads higher, slightly lower heat. If it reads lower, slightly raise heat.

Immediately set timer for 5 minutes again. After this 5 minutes, the thermometer should reach your third temperature level. If it reads higher or lower, adjust heat as before.

Stir constantly now and watch thermometer closely. In about 5 minutes, when thermometer reaches your EXACT finish temperature, IMMEDIATELY REMOVE FROM HEAT. Remove thermometer.

POUR INTO STIRRING PAN: Do not scrape cooking pan. Let fudge cool at room temperature for 5 minutes. Add remaining butter, vanilla extract and black walnuts.

BEGIN STIRRING: Use a clean sturdy spoon. Stir in an easy, steady manner. Do not beat or use an electric mixer. Scrape sides and all parts of pan. Fudge thickens and

holds its own shape in 4 to 10 minutes. TO KNOW IF FUDGE HAS THICKENED ENOUGH: Stop stirring. Count off 5 seconds. If fudge is still spreading out, resume stirring. Repeat until fudge holds its shape. WITHOUT A MOMENT'S DELAY, SCOOP FUDGE ONTO PLASTIC WRAP, USING THE SPATULA. Cool. Wrap tightly. Fudge tastes best after it has aged for 12 hours.

Opposite: Chocolate Black Walnut Fudge (p. 24)

CHOCOLATE COFFEE FUDGE

MAKES 1 POUND

INGREDIENTS

2 cups (450 g) sugar
1 cup (240 mL) milk
½ cup (45 g) cocoa (regular type such as Hershey's)
or 2½ ounces (75 g) unsweetened baking chocolate
3 tablespoons light corn syrup
¼ teaspoon salt
3 tablespoons (42 g) butter
1½ tablespoons instant coffee granules
2 tablespoons (28 g) butter, cut into several pieces
1 teaspoon vanilla extract
Optional: ½ cup (60 g) nuts

The coffee flavor really comes through in this fudge, but only after it has aged for 2 or 3 days; until then, it is fairly mild.

Find your finish temperature on page 14.

Set out on countertop stirring pan, 20-inch sheet of plastic wrap, spatula, timer or clock, and paper and pencil.

Combine sugar, milk, cocoa or chocolate, corn syrup, salt, 3 tablespoons butter and coffee in cooking pan. Place thermometer in pan with bulb ½ inch off the bottom. Leave in place until fudge is done. Turn heat to medium high. On a gas stove, look at flame at eye level. Turn flame to highest point, then back to medium; carefully adjust to medium high. On a large electric burner, medium heat may be appropriate. Stir to mix well.

When your first temperature level is reached, set a timer for 5 minutes (or jot down the time and watch a clock). Stir frequently or constantly if your

pan is thin. Scrape sides and bottom of pan as you stir. After 5 minutes, thermometer should reach your second temperature level. If it reads higher, slightly lower heat. If it reads lower, slightly raise heat.

Immediately set timer for 5 minutes again. After this 5 minutes, the thermometer should reach your third temperature level. If it reads higher or lower, adjust heat as before.

Stir constantly now and watch thermometer closely. In about 5 minutes, when thermometer reaches your EXACT finish temperature, IMMEDIATELY REMOVE FROM HEAT. Remove thermometer.

POUR INTO STIRRING PAN: Do not scrape cooking pan. Let fudge cool at room temperature for 5 minutes. Add remaining butter, vanilla extract and nuts.

BEGIN STIRRING: Use a clean sturdy spoon. Stir in an easy, steady manner. Do not beat or use an electric mixer. Scrape sides and all

parts of pan. Fudge thickens and holds its own shape in 4 to 10 minutes. TO KNOW IF FUDGE HAS THICKENED ENOUGH: Stop stirring. Count off 5 seconds. If fudge is still spreading out, resume stirring. Repeat until fudge holds its shape. WITHOUT A MOMENT'S DELAY, SCOOP FUDGE ONTO PLASTIC WRAP, USING THE SPATULA. Cool. Wrap tightly.

CHOCOLATE FUDGE MADE WITH DUTCH PROCESS COCOA

MAKES 1 POUND

INGREDIENTS

2 cups (450 g) sugar
1 cup (240 mL) milk
½ cup (45 g) Dutch process cocoa
(regular type such as Hershey's)
or 2½ ounces (75 g) unsweetened
baking chocolate
¼ teaspoon salt
3 tablespoons (42 g) butter
Optional: ¾ teaspoon instant
coffee granules
2 tablespoons (28 g) butter, cut
into several pieces
1 teaspoon vanilla extract
Optional: ½ cup (60 g) nuts
and/or dried fruit

Find your finish temperature on page 14.

Set out on countertop stirring pan, 20-inch sheet of plastic wrap, spatula, timer or clock, and paper and pencil.

Combine sugar, milk, cocoa or chocolate, salt, 3 tablespoons butter and coffee in cooking pan. Place thermometer in pan with bulb ½ inch off the bottom. Leave in place until fudge is done. Turn heat to medium high. On a gas stove, look at flame at eye level. Turn flame to highest point, then back to medium; carefully adjust to medium high. On a large electric burner, medium heat may be appropriate. Stir to mix well.

When your first temperature level is reached, set a timer for 5 minutes (or jot down the time and watch a clock). Stir frequently or constantly if your pan is thin. Scrape sides and bottom of pan as you stir. After 5 minutes, thermometer should reach your second temperature level. If it reads higher, slightly lower heat. If it reads lower, slightly raise heat.

Immediately set timer for 5 minutes again. After this 5 minutes, the thermometer should reach your third temperature level. If it reads higher or lower, adjust heat as before.

Stir constantly now and watch thermometer closely. In about 5 minutes, when thermometer reaches your EXACT finish temperature, IMMEDIATELY REMOVE FROM HEAT. Remove thermometer.

POUR INTO STIRRING PAN: Do not scrape cooking pan. Let fudge cool at room temperature for 5 minutes. Add remaining butter, vanilla extract and nuts.

BEGIN STIRRING: Use a clean sturdy spoon. Stir in an easy, steady manner. Do not beat or use an electric mixer. Scrape sides and all parts of pan. Fudge thickens and holds its own shape in 4 to 10 minutes. TO KNOW IF FUDGE HAS THICKENED ENOUGH: Stop stirring. Count off 5 seconds. If

fudge is still spreading out, resume stirring. Repeat until fudge holds its shape. WITHOUT A MOMENT'S DELAY, SCOOP FUDGE ONTO PLASTIC WRAP, USING THE SPATULA. Cool. Wrap tightly.SPATULA. Cool. Wrap tightly. Fudge tastes best after it has aged for 12 hours.

Note

You may substitute Dutch process cocoa for regular cocoa in these recipes: Black Walnut (page 24), Coconut Pecan (page 22), Mint (page 22), Sour Cream (page 30), Peanut Butter (page 22), and Smith College (page 34). Omit corn syrup.

CHOCOLATE SOUR CREAM FUDGE

MAKES 1 POUND

INGREDIENTS

2 cups (450 g) sugar
½ cup (45 g) cocoa (regular type such as Hershey's)
or 2½ ounces (75 g) unsweetened baking chocolate
½ cup (114 g) commercial sour cream
½ cup (120 mL) water
3 tablespoons light corn syrup
¼ teaspoon salt
3 tablespoons (42 g) butter
2 tablespoons (28 g) butter, cut into several pieces
1 teaspoon vanilla extract
Optional: ½ cup (60 g) nuts and/or dried fruit

This is very smooth and dark, with a lingering, pleasant sour cream after-taste.

Find your finish temperature on page 14.

Set out on countertop stirring pan, 20-inch sheet of plastic wrap, spatula, timer or clock, and paper and pencil.

Combine sugar, cocoa or chocolate, sour cream, water, corn syrup, salt, 3 tablespoons butter and coffee in cooking pan. Place thermometer in pan with bulb ½ inch off the bottom. Leave in place until fudge is done. Turn heat to medium high. On a gas stove, look at flame at eye level. Turn flame to highest point, then back to medium; carefully adjust to medium high. On a large electric burner, medium heat may be appropriate. Stir to mix well.

When your first temperature level is reached, set a timer for 5 minutes (or jot down the time and watch a clock). Stir frequently or constantly if your

pan is thin. Scrape sides and bottom of pan as you stir. After 5 minutes, thermometer should reach your second temperature level. If it reads higher, slightly lower heat. If it reads lower, slightly raise heat.

Immediately set timer for 5 minutes again. After this 5 minutes, the thermometer should reach your third temperature level. If it reads higher or lower, adjust heat as before.

Stir constantly now and watch thermometer closely. In about 5 minutes, when thermometer reaches your EXACT finish temperature, IMMEDIATELY REMOVE FROM HEAT. Remove thermometer.

POUR INTO STIRRING PAN: Do not scrape cooking pan. Let fudge cool at room temperature for 5 minutes. Add remaining butter, vanilla extract and nuts or fruit.

BEGIN STIRRING: Use a clean sturdy spoon. Stir in an easy, steady manner. Do not beat or use an electric mixer. Scrape sides and all parts of pan. Fudge thickens and holds its own shape in 4 to 10 minutes. TO KNOW IF FUDGE HAS THICKENED ENOUGH: Stop stirring. Count off 5 seconds. If fudge is still spreading out, resume stirring. Repeat until fudge holds its shape. WITHOUT A MOMENT'S DELAY, SCOOP FUDGE ONTO PLASTIC WRAP, USING THE SPATULA. Cool. Wrap tightly. Fudge tastes best after it has aged for 12 hours.

EASY CHOCOLATE FUDGE

MAKES 1 POUND

INGREDIENTS

2 cups (450 g) sugar
1 cup (240 mL) milk
½ cup (45 g) cocoa (regular type
such as Hershey's)
or 2½ ounces (75 g)
unsweetened baking chocolate
¼ teaspoon salt
3 tablespoons (42 g) butter
Optional: ¾ teaspoon instant
coffee granules
2 tablespoons (28 g) butter, cut
into several pieces
1 teaspoon vanilla extract
Optional: ½ cup (60 g) nuts
and/or dried fruit

This is easy because you don't time the cooking.

Find your FIRST temperature level on page 14. Add 22°F (12°C). This is your finish temperature.

Set out on countertop stirring pan, 20-inch sheet of plastic wrap, and spatula.

Combine sugar, milk, cocoa or chocolate, salt, 3 tablespoons butter and coffee in cooking pan. Place thermometer in pan with bulb ½ inch off the bottom. Leave in place until fudge is done. Turn heat to medium high. On a gas stove, look at flame at eye level. Turn flame to highest point, then back to medium; carefully adjust to medium high. On a large electric burner, medium heat may be appropriate.

Cook, stirring frequently, until temperature is within 5 degrees of your finish temperature. Watch thermometer closely, stirring constantly, until your EXACT finish temperature is reached.

IMMEDIATELY REMOVE FROM HEAT. Remove thermometer.

POUR INTO STIRRING PAN: Do not scrape cooking pan. Let fudge cool at room temperature for 5 minutes. Add remaining butter, vanilla extract and nuts or fruit.

BEGIN STIRRING: Use a clean sturdy spoon. Stir in an easy, steady manner. Do not beat or use an electric mixer. Scrape sides and all parts of pan. Fudge thickens and holds its own shape in 4 to 10 minutes. TO KNOW IF FUDGE HAS THICKENED ENOUGH: Stop stirring. Count off 5 seconds. If fudge is still spreading out, resume stirring. Repeat until fudge holds its shape. WITHOUT A MOMENT'S DELAY, SCOOP FUDGE ONTO PLASTIC WRAP, USING THE SPATULA. Cool. Wrap tightly. Fudge tastes best after it has aged for 12 hours.

Note:

You may make Easy Chocolate Fudge using the ingredients in any recipe except Honey, Molasses, or Smith College Fudge. Omit corn syrup.

SMITH COLLEGE FUDGE

MAKES 1 POUND

INGREDIENTS

2¼ cups packed (450 g) light
brown sugar
1 cup (240 mL) milk
½ cup (45 g) cocoa (regular type
such as Hershey's)
or 2½ ounces (75 g) unsweetened
baking chocolate
¼ teaspoon salt
3 tablespoons (42 g) butter
2 tablespoons (28 g) butter, cut
into several pieces
1 teaspoon vanilla extract
Optional: ½ cup (60 g) nuts
and/or dried fruit

Girls at Smith College made this in their rooms almost 100 years ago. They flavored their fudge with brown sugar. The result is not quite as sweet as fudge made with white sugar.

Find your finish temperature on page 14.

Set out on countertop stirring pan, 20-inch sheet of plastic wrap, spatula, timer or clock, and paper and pencil.

Combine sugar, milk, cocoa or chocolate, salt, and 3 tablespoons butter in cooking pan. Place thermometer in pan with bulb ½ inch off the bottom. Leave in place until fudge is done. Turn heat to medium high. On a gas stove, look at flame at eye level. Turn flame to highest point, then back to medium; carefully adjust to medium high. On a large electric burner, medium heat may be appropriate. Stir to mix well.

When your first temperature level is reached, set a timer for 5 minutes (or jot down the time and watch a clock).

Stir frequently or constantly if your pan is thin. Scrape sides and bottom of pan as you stir. After 5 minutes, thermometer should reach your second temperature level. If it reads higher, slightly lower heat. If it reads lower, slightly raise heat.

Immediately set timer for 5 minutes again. After this 5 minutes, the thermometer should reach your third temperature level. If it reads higher or lower, adjust heat as before.

Stir constantly now and watch thermometer closely. In about 5 minutes, when thermometer reaches your EXACT finish temperature, IMMEDIATELY REMOVE FROM HEAT. Remove thermometer.

POUR INTO STIRRING PAN: Do not scrape cooking pan. Let fudge cool at room temperature for 5 minutes. Add remaining butter, vanilla extract and nuts or fruit.

BEGIN STIRRING: Use a clean sturdy spoon. Stir in an easy, steady manner. Do not beat or use an electric mixer. Scrape sides and all parts of pan. Fudge thickens and holds its own shape in 4 to 10 minutes. TO KNOW IF FUDGE HAS THICKENED ENOUGH: Stop stirring. Count off 5 seconds. If fudge is still spreading out, resume stirring. Repeat until fudge holds its shape. WITHOUT A MOMENT'S DELAY, SCOOP FUDGE ONTO PLASTIC WRAP, USING THE SPATULA. Cool. Wrap tightly. Fudge tastes best after it has aged for 12 hours.

CREME FUDGES

VANILLA CREME FUDGES
(WHITE FUDGE, BLONDE FUDGE OR OPERA CREME)

MAKES 1 POUND

INGREDIENTS

2 cups (450 g) sugar
1 cup (240 mL milk)
2 tablespoons light corn syrup
¼ teaspoon salt
2 tablespoons (28 g) butter, cut
into several pieces
1 teaspoon vanilla
Optional: ½ cup (60 g) nuts or
dried fruit

Some think this is the best. The ingredients are deceptively simple; the flavor is pure vanilla.

Find your finish temperature on page 14.

Set out on countertop stirring pan, 20-inch sheet of plastic wrap, spatula, timer or clock, and paper and pencil.

Combine sugar, milk, corn syrup and salt in cooking pan. Place thermometer in pan with bulb ½ inch off the bottom. Leave in place until fudge is done. Turn heat to medium high. On a gas stove, look at flame at eye level. Turn flame to highest point, then back to medium; carefully adjust to medium high. On a large electric burner, medium heat may be appropriate. Stir to mix well.

When your first temperature level is reached, set a timer for 5 minutes (or jot down the time and watch a clock). Stir frequently or constantly if your pan is thin. Scrape sides and bottom of pan as you stir. After 5 minutes,

thermometer should reach your second temperature level. If it reads higher, slightly lower heat. If it reads lower, slightly raise heat.

Immediately set timer for 5 minutes again. After this 5 minutes, the thermometer should reach your third temperature level. If it reads higher or lower, adjust heat as before.

Stir constantly now and watch thermometer closely. In about 5 minutes, when thermometer reaches your EXACT finish temperature, IMMEDIATELY REMOVE FROM HEAT. Remove thermometer.

POUR INTO STIRRING PAN: Do not scrape cooking pan. Let fudge cool at room temperature for 5 minutes. Add butter, vanilla extract and nuts or fruit.

BEGIN STIRRING: Use a clean sturdy spoon. Stir in an easy, steady manner. Do not beat or use an electric mixer. Scrape sides and all parts of pan. Fudge thickens and holds its own shape in 4 to 10 minutes. TO KNOW IF FUDGE HAS THICKENED ENOUGH: Stop stirring. Count off 5 seconds. If fudge is still spreading out, resume stirring. Repeat until fudge holds its shape. WITHOUT A MOMENT'S DELAY, SCOOP FUDGE ONTO PLASTIC WRAP, USING THE SPATULA. Cool. Wrap tightly. Fudge tastes best after it has aged for 12 hours.

Variation

VANILLA RUM CREME FUDGE
Add ¼ cup (60 mL) rum,[*] dark preferred, and 2 tablespoons (28 g) butter to the cooking pan.

---

[*]Alcohol may cause the cooking syrup to foam to the top of the pan. Lower heat until foaming subsides.

BROWN SUGAR CREME FUDGE (PENUCHE)

MAKES 1 POUND

INGREDIENTS

1 pound (2¼ cups firmly
packed/450 g) light brown sugar
1 cup (240 mL) milk
1 tablespoon butter
¼ teaspoon salt
2 tablespoons (28 g) butter, cut
into several pieces
1 teaspoon vanilla extract
½ to 1 cup (60 to 120 g) whole
pecans

For more than 100 years Southern cooks have combined brown sugar and their native pecans to make their famous pralines and penuche. Here is a creamy smooth version of those old favorites.

Find your finish temperature on page 14.

Set out on countertop stirring pan, 20-inch sheet of plastic wrap, spatula, timer or clock, and paper and pencil.

Combine sugar, milk, 1 tablespoon butter and salt in cooking pan. Place thermometer in pan with bulb ½ inch off the bottom. Leave in place until fudge is done. Turn heat to medium high. On a gas stove, look at flame at eye level. Turn flame to highest point, then back to medium; carefully adjust to medium high. On a large electric burner, medium heat may be appropriate. Stir to mix well.

When your first temperature level is reached, set a timer for 5 minutes (or jot down the time and watch a clock).

Opposite: Brown Sugar Creme Fudge

Stir frequently or constantly if your pan is thin. Scrape sides and bottom of pan as you stir. After 5 minutes, thermometer should reach your second temperature level. If it reads higher, slightly lower heat. If it reads lower, slightly raise heat.

Immediately set timer for 5 minutes again. After this 5 minutes, the thermometer should reach your third temperature level. If it reads higher or lower, adjust heat as before.

Stir constantly now and watch thermometer closely. In about 5 minutes, when thermometer reaches your EXACT finish temperature, IMMEDIATELY REMOVE FROM HEAT. Remove thermometer.

POUR INTO STIRRING PAN: Do not scrape cooking pan. Let fudge cool at room temperature for 5 minutes. Add remaining butter, vanilla extract and pecans.

BEGIN STIRRING: Use a clean sturdy spoon. Stir in an easy, steady manner. Do not beat or use an electric mixer. Scrape sides and all parts of pan. Fudge thickens and holds its own shape in 4 to 10 minutes. TO KNOW IF FUDGE HAS THICKENED ENOUGH: Stop stirring. Count off 5 seconds. If fudge is still spreading out, resume stirring. Repeat until fudge holds its shape. WITHOUT A MOMENT'S DELAY, SCOOP FUDGE ONTO PLASTIC WRAP, USING THE SPATULA. Cool. Wrap tightly. Fudge tastes best after it has aged for 12 hours.

Variation

BUTTERSCOTCH CREME FUDGE

Old-fashioned butterscotch is a blend of brown sugar and butter.

Reduce light brown sugar to 1 cup packed (225 g). Add 1 cup (225 g) granulated sugar and 1 tablespoon light corn syrup to cooking pan. Increase butter in cooking pan to 4 tablespoons (60 g). Omit salt.

Opposite: Vanilla Creme Fudge with Dried Cherries (p. 38)

41

BUTTER CREME FUDGE

MAKES 1 POUND

INGREDIENTS
2 cups (450 g) sugar
1 cup (240 mL) milk
4 tablespoons (60 g) butter
2 tablespoons light corn syrup
1/8 teaspoon salt
2 tablespoons (28 g) butter, cut
into several pieces
1 teaspoon vanilla extract
Optional: 1/2 cup (60 g) nuts or
dried coconut

An incredibly rich blend of butter and vanilla.

Find your finish temperature on page 14.

Set out on countertop stirring pan, 20-inch sheet of plastic wrap, spatula, timer or clock, and paper and pencil.

BEGIN COOKING: Combine sugar, milk, 4 tablespoons butter, corn syrup and salt in cooking pan. Place thermometer in pan with bulb 1/2 inch off the bottom. Leave in place until fudge is done. Turn heat to medium high. On a gas stove, look at flame at eye level. Turn flame to highest point, then back to medium; carefully adjust to medium high. On a large electric burner, medium heat may be appropriate. Stir to mix well.

When your first temperature level is reached, set a timer for 5 minutes (or jot down the time and watch a clock). Stir frequently or constantly if your pan is thin. Scrape sides and bottom of pan as you stir. After 5 minutes,

thermometer should reach your second temperature level. If it reads higher, slightly lower heat. If it reads lower, slightly raise heat.

Immediately set timer for 5 minutes again. After this 5 minutes, the thermometer should reach your third temperature level. If it reads higher or lower, adjust heat as before.

Stir constantly now and watch thermometer closely. In about 5 minutes, when thermometer reaches your EXACT finish temperature, IMMEDIATELY REMOVE FROM HEAT. Remove thermometer.

POUR INTO STIRRING PAN: Do not scrape cooking pan. Let fudge cool at room temperature for 5 minutes. Add remaining butter, vanilla extract and nuts or coconut.

BEGIN STIRRING: Use a clean sturdy spoon. Stir in an easy, steady manner. Do not beat or use an electric mixer. Scrape sides and all parts of pan. Fudge thickens and holds its own shape in 4 to 10

minutes. TO KNOW IF FUDGE HAS THICKENED ENOUGH: Stop stirring. Count off 5 seconds. If fudge is still spreading out, resume stirring. Repeat until fudge holds its shape. WITHOUT A MOMENT'S DELAY, SCOOP FUDGE ONTO PLASTIC WRAP, USING THE SPATULA. Cool. Wrap tightly. Fudge tastes best after it has aged for 12 hours.

Variations

BUTTER MINT CREME FUDGE
Buttery, melt-in-your-mouth mint. Substitute 1 teaspoon peppermint extract for vanilla.

BUTTER RUM CREME FUDGE
Add ¼ cup (60 mL) rum,* dark preferred, to the cooking pan. Reduce butter in cooking pan to 2 tablespoons (28 g)

---

*Alcohol may cause the cooking syrup to foam to the top of the pan. Lower heat until foaming subsides.

MOLASSES CREME FUDGE

MAKES 1 POUND

INGREDIENTS

2 cups (450 g) sugar
½ cup (120 mL) water
½ cup (114 g) commercial sour
cream
2 tablespoons unsulphured
molasses
¼ teaspoon baking soda
¼ teaspoon salt
2 tablespoons (28 g) butter, cut
into several pieces
1 teaspoon vanilla extract
Optional: ½ cup (60 g) nuts or
dried coconut

A mild molasses taste very similar to Brown Sugar Creme Fudge (page 40). Pecans are almost a must in this, they go so well.

Find your finish temperature on page 14.

Set out on countertop stirring pan, 20-inch sheet of plastic wrap, spatula, timer or clock, and paper and pencil.

Combine sugar, water, sour cream, molasses, baking soda and salt in cooking pan. Place thermometer in pan with bulb ½ inch off the bottom. Leave in place until fudge is done. Turn heat to medium high.* On a gas stove, look at flame at eye level. Turn flame to highest point, then back to medium; carefully adjust to medium high. On a large electric burner, medium heat may be appropriate. Stir to mix well.

When your first temperature level is reached, set a timer for 5 minutes (or

---

**Baking soda may cause the cooking syrup to foam to the top of the pan. Lower heat until foaming subsides.*

*jot down the time and watch a clock).
Stir frequently or constantly if your
pan is thin. Scrape sides and bottom
of pan as you stir. After 5 minutes,
thermometer should reach your second
temperature level. If it reads higher,
slightly lower heat. If it reads lower,
slightly raise heat.*

*Immediately set timer for 5 minutes
again. After this 5 minutes, the
thermometer should reach your third
temperature level. If it reads higher or
lower, adjust heat as before.*

*Stir constantly now and watch
thermometer closely. In about 5
minutes, when thermometer reaches
your EXACT finish temperature,
IMMEDIATELY REMOVE FROM
HEAT. Remove thermometer.*

*POUR INTO STIRRING PAN: Do
not scrape cooking pan. Let fudge
cool at room temperature for 5
minutes. Add butter, vanilla extract,
and nuts or coconut.*

*BEGIN STIRRING: Use a clean
sturdy spoon. Stir in an easy, steady*

*manner. Do not beat or use an
electric mixer. Scrape sides and all
parts of pan. Fudge thickens and
holds its own shape in 4 to 10
minutes. TO KNOW IF FUDGE
HAS THICKENED ENOUGH: Stop
stirring. Count off 5 seconds. If
fudge is still spreading out, resume
stirring. Repeat until fudge holds its
shape. WITHOUT A MOMENT'S
DELAY, SCOOP FUDGE ONTO
PLASTIC WRAP, USING THE
SPATULA. Cool. Wrap tightly.
Fudge tastes best after it has aged for
12 hours.*

MAPLE CREME FUDGE

MAKES 1 POUND

INGREDIENTS

2 cups (450 g) sugar
1 cup (240 mL) milk
2 tablespoons light corn syrup
¼ teaspoon salt
2 tablespoons (28 g) butter, cut
into several pieces
1 teaspoon maple extract
Optional: ½ cup (60 g) nuts

Find your finish temperature on page 14.

Set out on countertop stirring pan, 20-inch sheet of plastic wrap, spatula, timer or clock, and paper and pencil.

BEGIN COOKING: Combine sugar, milk, corn syrup and salt in cooking pan. Place thermometer in pan with bulb ½ inch off the bottom. Leave in place until fudge is done. Turn heat to medium high. On a gas stove, look at flame at eye level. Turn flame to highest point, then back to medium; carefully adjust to medium high. On a large electric burner, medium heat may be appropriate. Stir to mix well.

When your first temperature level is reached, set a timer for 5 minutes (or jot down the time and watch a clock). Stir frequently or constantly if your pan is thin. Scrape sides and bottom of pan as you stir. After 5 minutes, thermometer should reach your second temperature level. If it reads higher, slightly lower heat. If it reads lower, slightly raise heat.

Immediately set timer for 5 minutes again. After this 5 minutes, the thermometer should reach your third temperature level. If it reads higher or lower, adjust heat as before.

Stir constantly now and watch thermometer closely. In about 5 minutes, when thermometer reaches your EXACT finish temperature, IMMEDIATELY REMOVE FROM HEAT. Remove thermometer.

POUR INTO STIRRING PAN: Do not scrape cooking pan. Let fudge cool at room temperature for 5 minutes. Add butter, maple extract and nuts.

BEGIN STIRRING: Use a clean sturdy spoon. Stir in an easy, steady manner. Do not beat or use an electric mixer. Scrape sides and all parts of pan. Fudge thickens and holds its own shape in 4 to 10 minutes. TO KNOW IF FUDGE HAS THICKENED ENOUGH: Stop stirring. Count off 5 seconds. If fudge is still spreading out, resume stirring. Repeat until fudge holds its

shape. WITHOUT A MOMENT'S DELAY, SCOOP FUDGE ONTO PLASTIC WRAP, USING THE SPATULA. Cool. Wrap tightly. Fudge tastes best after it has aged for 12 hours.

Variation

MAPLE RUM CREME FUDGE
Add 2 tablespoons rum, dark preferred, to the cooking pan.*

Alcohol may cause the cooking syrup to foam to the top of the pan. Lower heat until foaming subsides.

47

PURE MAPLE CREME FUDGE

MAKES 1 POUND

INGREDIENTS

2 cups (480 mL) pure maple
syrup
1 cup (240 mL) heavy cream

Only two ingredients. An elegant fudge.

Set out on the countertop stirring pan, 20-inch sheet of plastic wrap, and spatula.

Find your first temperature level on page 14. Add 26°F (14°C). This is your finish temperature. It is not necessary to time the cooking.

Combine sugar and cream in cooking pan.

Place candy thermometer in cooking pan with bulb ½ inch off the bottom. Leave in place until fudge is done. Turn heat to medium high. Cook, stirring frequently, until temperature is within 5° of your finish temperature. Watch thermometer closely, stirring constantly, until your EXACT finish temperature is reached. IMMEDIATELY REMOVE FROM HEAT. Remove thermometer.

POUR INTO STIRRING PAN: Do not scrape cooking pan. Let fudge cool at room temperature for 5 minutes.

BEGIN STIRRING: Use a clean sturdy spoon. Stir in an easy, steady manner. Do not beat or use an electric mixer. Scrape sides and all parts of pan. Fudge thickens and holds its own shape in 4 to 10 minutes. TO KNOW IF FUDGE HAS THICKENED ENOUGH: Stop stirring. Count off 5 seconds. If fudge is still spreading out, resume stirring. Repeat until fudge holds its shape. WITHOUT A MOMENT'S DELAY, SCOOP FUDGE ONTO PLASTIC WRAP, USING THE SPATULA. Cool. Wrap tightly. Fudge tastes best after it has aged for 12 hours.

ALMOND CREME FUDGE

MAKES 1 POUND

INGREDIENTS

2 cups (450 g) sugar
1 cup (240 mL) milk
2 tablespoons light corn syrup
¼ teaspoon salt
2 tablespoons (28 g) butter, cut
into several pieces
1 teaspoon vanilla extract
½ teaspoon almond extract
Optional: ½ cup (60 g) roasted,
slivered almonds

Almond and vanilla flavors blend wonderfully. Here the prevalent taste is almond, with a vanilla undertone.

Find your finish temperature on page 14.

Set out on countertop stirring pan, 20-inch sheet of plastic wrap, spatula, timer or clock, and paper and pencil.

Combine sugar, milk, corn syrup and salt in cooking pan. Place thermometer in pan with bulb ½ inch off the bottom. Leave in place until fudge is done. Turn heat to medium high. On a gas stove, look at flame at eye level. Turn flame to highest point, then back to medium; carefully adjust to medium high. On a large electric burner, medium heat may be appropriate. Stir to mix well.

When your first temperature level is reached, set a timer for 5 minutes (or jot down the time and watch a clock). Stir frequently or constantly if your pan is thin. Scrape sides and bottom of pan as you stir. After 5 minutes, thermometer should reach your second temperature level. *If it reads higher, slightly lower heat. If it reads lower, slightly raise heat.*

Immediately set timer for 5 minutes again. After this 5 minutes, the thermometer should reach your third temperature level. If it reads higher or lower, adjust heat as before.

Stir constantly now and watch thermometer closely. In about 5 minutes, when thermometer reaches your EXACT finish temperature, IMMEDIATELY REMOVE FROM HEAT. Remove thermometer.

POUR INTO STIRRING PAN: Do not scrape cooking pan. Let fudge cool at room temperature for 5 minutes. Add butter, extracts and almonds.

BEGIN STIRRING: Use a clean sturdy spoon. Stir in an easy, steady manner. Do not beat or use an electric mixer. Scrape sides and all parts of pan. Fudge thickens and holds its own shape in 4 to 10 minutes. TO KNOW IF FUDGE HAS THICKENED ENOUGH: Stop

stirring. Count off 5 seconds. If fudge is still spreading out, resume stirring. Repeat until fudge holds its shape. WITHOUT A MOMENT'S DELAY, SCOOP FUDGE ONTO PLASTIC WRAP, USING THE SPATULA. Cool. Wrap tightly. Fudge tastes best after it has aged for 12 hours.

Variations

ALMOND BUTTER CREME FUDGE
Almond butter is just like peanut butter, except it's ground roasted almonds. You can buy it or grind your own.

Add ¼ cup (65 g) crunchy or smooth almond butter to the stirring pan.

AMARETTO CREME FUDGE
A delicate flavor that takes two days to fully develop.

Add ¼ cup (60 mL) amaretto liqueur* to the cooking pan. Omit vanilla.

---

*Alcohol may cause the cooking syrup to foam to the top of the pan. Lower heat until foaming subsides.

51

COCONUT CREME FUDGE

MAKES 1 POUND

INGREDIENTS

2 cups (450 g) sugar
¾ cup (180 mL) canned evaporated milk
¼ cup (60 mL) water
2 tablespoons light corn syrup
¼ teaspoon salt
2 tablespoons (28 g) butter, cut into several pieces
1 teaspoon vanilla extract
1 teaspoon coconut extract
Optional: ½ cup (60 g) dried coconut

Make this with your own fresh coconut or use the commerical kind. This is also very flavorful even without the coconut.

Find your finish temperature on page 14.

Set out on countertop stirring pan, 20-inch sheet of plastic wrap, spatula, timer or clock, and paper and pencil.

BEGIN COOKING: Combine sugar, milk, water, corn syrup and salt in cooking pan. Place thermometer in pan with bulb ½ inch off the bottom. Leave in place until fudge is done. Turn heat to medium high. On a gas stove, look at flame at eye level. Turn flame to highest point, then back to medium; carefully adjust to medium high. On a large electric burner, medium heat may be appropriate. Stir to mix well.

When your first temperature level is reached, set a timer for 5 minutes (or jot down the time and watch a clock). Stir frequently or constantly if your

pan is thin. Scrape sides and bottom of pan as you stir. After 5 minutes, thermometer should reach your second temperature level. If it reads higher, slightly lower heat. If it reads lower, slightly raise heat.

Immediately set timer for 5 minutes again. After this 5 minutes, the thermometer should reach your third temperature level. If it reads higher or lower, adjust heat as before.

Stir constantly now and watch thermometer closely. In about 5 minutes, when thermometer reaches your EXACT finish temperature, IMMEDIATELY REMOVE FROM HEAT. Remove thermometer.

POUR INTO STIRRING PAN: Do not scrape cooking pan. Let fudge cool at room temperature for 5 minutes. Add butter, extracts and coconut.

BEGIN STIRRING: Use a clean sturdy spoon. Stir in an easy, steady manner. Do not beat or use an electric mixer. Scrape sides and all

parts of pan. Fudge thickens and holds its own shape in 4 to 10 minutes. TO KNOW IF FUDGE HAS THICKENED ENOUGH: Stop stirring. Count off 5 seconds. If fudge is still spreading out, resume stirring. Repeat until fudge holds its shape. WITHOUT A MOMENT'S DELAY, SCOOP FUDGE ONTO PLASTIC WRAP, USING THE SPATULA. Cool. Wrap tightly. Fudge tastes best after it has aged for 12 hours.

Variation

COCONUT RUM CREME FUDGE
Add ¼ cup (60 mL) rum,* dark preferred, to the cooking pan. Omit vanilla.

---

*Alcohol may cause the cooking syrup to foam to the top of the pan. Lower heat until foaming subsides.

PEANUT BUTTER CREME FUDGE

MAKES 1 POUND

INGREDIENTS

2 cups (450 g) sugar
1 cup (240 mL) milk
2 tablespoons light corn syrup
¼ teaspoon salt
2 tablespoons (28 g) butter, cut
into several pieces
1 teaspoon vanilla extract
¼ cup (65 g) crunchy or smooth
peanut butter
Optional: ½ cup (60 g) peanuts

This is wonderful. You can knead it into any shape and press salted peanuts into the top.

Find your finish temperature on page 14.

Set out on countertop stirring pan, 20-inch sheet of plastic wrap, spatula, timer or clock, and paper and pencil.

Combine sugar, milk, corn syrup and salt in cooking pan. Place thermometer in pan with bulb ½ inch off the bottom. Leave in place until fudge is done. Turn heat to medium high. On a gas stove, look at flame at eye level. Turn flame to highest point, then back to medium; carefully adjust to medium high. On a large electric burner, medium heat may be appropriate. Stir to mix well.

When your first temperature level is reached, set a timer for 5 minutes (or jot down the time and watch a clock). Stir frequently or constantly if your pan is thin. Scrape sides and bottom of pan as you stir. After 5 minutes,

thermometer should reach your second temperature level. If it reads higher, slightly lower heat. If it reads lower, slightly raise heat.

Immediately set timer for 5 minutes again. After this 5 minutes, the thermometer should reach your third temperature level. If it reads higher or lower, adjust heat as before.

Stir constantly now and watch thermometer closely. In about 5 minutes, when thermometer reaches your EXACT finish temperature, IMMEDIATELY REMOVE FROM HEAT. Remove thermometer.

POUR INTO STIRRING PAN: Do not scrape cooking pan. Let fudge cool at room temperature for 5 minutes. Add butter, vanilla extract, peanut butter and peanuts.

BEGIN STIRRING: Use a clean sturdy spoon. Stir in an easy, steady manner. Do not beat or use an electric mixer. Scrape sides and all parts of pan. Fudge thickens and holds its own shape in 4 to 10

minutes. TO KNOW IF FUDGE HAS THICKENED ENOUGH: Stop stirring. Count off 5 seconds. If fudge is still spreading out, resume stirring. Repeat until fudge holds its shape. WITHOUT A MOMENT'S DELAY, SCOOP FUDGE ONTO PLASTIC WRAP, USING THE SPATULA. Cool. Wrap tightly. Fudge tastes best after it has aged for 12 hours.

Variation

PEANUT BUTTER BANANA CREME FUDGE
Substitute 2 teaspoons banana extract for vanilla.

BILL'S BLACK WALNUT CREME FUDGE

MAKES 1 POUND

INGREDIENTS

2 cups (450 g) sugar
1 cup (240 mL) milk
2 tablespoons light corn syrup
¼ teaspoon salt
2 tablespoons (28 g) butter, cut
into several pieces
1 teaspoon black walnut extract
½ to 1 cup (60 to 120 g) black
walnuts

My brother-in-law Bill Myerly likes *Black Walnut Fudge* so thick with walnuts that the candy really only serves to hold the nuts together. If you love black walnuts as he does, that's not too much. To make Bill's fudge, add a good heaping cupful; otherwise, ½ cup will do nicely.

Find your finish temperature on page 14.

Set out on countertop stirring pan, 20-inch sheet of plastic wrap, spatula, timer or clock, and paper and pencil.

Combine sugar, milk, corn syrup and salt in cooking pan. Place thermometer in pan with bulb ½ inch off the bottom. Leave in place until fudge is done. Turn heat to medium high. On a gas stove, look at flame at eye level. Turn flame to highest point, then back to medium; carefully adjust to medium high. On a large electric burner, medium heat may be appropriate. Stir to mix well.

When your first temperature level is

Opposite: Bill's Black Walnut Creme Fudge

reached, set a timer for 5 minutes (or jot down the time and watch a clock). Stir frequently or constantly if your pan is thin. Scrape sides and bottom of pan as you stir. After 5 minutes, thermometer should reach your second temperature level. If it reads higher, slightly lower heat. If it reads lower, slightly raise heat.

Immediately set timer for 5 minutes again. After this 5 minutes, the thermometer should reach your third temperature level. If it reads higher or lower, adjust heat as before.

Stir constantly now and watch thermometer closely. In about 5 minutes, when thermometer reaches your EXACT finish temperature, IMMEDIATELY REMOVE FROM HEAT. Remove thermometer.

POUR INTO STIRRING PAN: Do not scrape cooking pan. Let fudge cool at room temperature for 5 minutes. Add butter, extract and black walnuts.

BEGIN STIRRING: Use a clean sturdy spoon. Stir in an easy, steady manner. Do not beat or use an electric mixer. Scrape sides and all parts of pan. Fudge thickens and holds its own shape in 4 to 10 minutes. TO KNOW IF FUDGE HAS THICKENED ENOUGH: Stop stirring. Count off 5 seconds. If fudge is still spreading out, resume stirring. Repeat until fudge holds its shape. WITHOUT A MOMENT'S DELAY, SCOOP FUDGE ONTO PLASTIC WRAP, USING THE SPATULA. Cool. Wrap tightly. Fudge tastes best after it has aged for 12 hours.

Opposite: Butter Creme Fudge, top (p. 42)
Fruity Creme Fudge, below (p. 77)

57

BUTTERMILK CREME FUDGE

MAKES 1 POUND

INGREDIENTS

2 cups (450 g) sugar
1 cup (240 mL) buttermilk
(regular preferred, low-fat
acceptable)
2 tablespoons light corn syrup
¼ teaspoon baking soda
¼ teaspoon salt
2 tablespoons (28 g) butter, cut
into several pieces
1 teaspoon vanilla extract
Optional: ½ cup (60 g) nuts or
dried coconut

Pecans are great in this, especially when you use regular-type buttermilk.

Find your finish temperature on page 14.

Set out on countertop stirring pan, 20-inch sheet of plastic wrap, spatula, timer or clock, and paper and pencil.

BEGIN COOKING: Combine sugar, buttermilk, corn syrup, baking soda and salt in cooking pan. Place thermometer in pan with bulb ½ inch off the bottom. Leave in place until fudge is done. Turn heat to medium high. On a gas stove, look at flame at eye level. Turn flame to highest point, then back to medium; carefully adjust to medium high. On a large electric burner, medium heat may be appropriate. Stir to mix well.*

When your first temperature level is reached, set a timer for 5 minutes (or jot down the time and watch a clock).

Baking soda may cause the cooking syrup to foam to the top of the pan. Lower heat until foaming subsides.

Stir frequently or constantly if your pan is thin. Scrape sides and bottom of pan as you stir. After 5 minutes, thermometer should reach your second temperature level. If it reads higher, slightly lower heat. If it reads lower, slightly raise heat.

Immediately set timer for 5 minutes again. After this 5 minutes, the thermometer should reach your third temperature level. If it reads higher or lower, adjust heat as before.

Stir constantly now and watch thermometer closely. In about 5 minutes, when thermometer reaches your EXACT finish temperature, IMMEDIATELY REMOVE FROM HEAT. Remove thermometer.

POUR INTO STIRRING PAN: Do not scrape cooking pan. Let fudge cool at room temperature for 5 minutes. Add butter, vanilla extract and nuts or coconut.

BEGIN STIRRING: Use a clean sturdy spoon. Stir in an easy, steady manner. Do not beat or use an electric mixer. Scrape sides and all parts of pan. Fudge thickens and holds its own shape in 4 to 10 minutes. TO KNOW IF FUDGE HAS THICKENED ENOUGH: Stop stirring. Count off 5 seconds. If fudge is still spreading out, resume stirring. Repeat until fudge holds its shape. WITHOUT A MOMENT'S DELAY, SCOOP FUDGE ONTO PLASTIC WRAP, USING THE SPATULA. Cool. Wrap tightly. Fudge tastes best after it has aged for 12 hours.

CARAMEL CREME FUDGE
(BURNT SUGAR FUDGE OR OKLAHOMA BROWN CANDY)

MAKES 1 POUND

INGREDIENTS

1 cup (240 mL) milk
2 cups (450 g) sugar
3 tablespoons (42 g) butter
¼ teaspoon salt
2 tablespoons (28 g) butter, cut
into several pieces
1 teaspoon vanilla extract
Optional: ½ cup (60 g) nuts or
dried coconut

True caramel flavor comes from caramelized white sugar. Use a heavy cooking pan; caramelized sugar burns easily.

Find your first temperature level on page 14. Add 28°F (15°C). This is your finish temperature. It is not necessary to time the cooking. Set out on countertop stirring pan, 20-inch sheet of plastic wrap, and spatula.

Place candy thermometer in a small pan with milk. Heat until very hot. Remove pan from heat and set aside. Leave thermometer in pan to stay hot.

Place 1 cup (225 g) sugar in the large clean cooking pan. Caramelize sugar by turning heat to medium and stirring constantly until sugar melts to a light brown liquid and just starts to take on a slightly reddish hue. Immediately remove from heat.

Very slowly, just a few tablespoons at a time at first, and keeping your hands and arms clear of the top of the pan, pour the hot milk into the caramelized sugar, stirring constantly. The mixture will foam and create steam; use care to avoid burns. Add remaining 1 cup (225 g) sugar and 3 tablespoons butter and salt.

Set thermometer in cooking pan with bulb ½ inch off the bottom. Leave in place until fudge is done. Turn heat to medium. Caramel hardens when the milk is added and will slowly remelt again as it heats. Stir constantly until your finish temperature is reached; this will take between 10 and 15 minutes. Remove from heat. Remove thermometer.

POUR INTO STIRRING PAN: Do not scrape cooking pan. Let fudge cool at room temperature for 5 minutes. Add remaining 2 tablespoons butter, vanilla extract and nuts or coconut.

BEGIN STIRRING: Use a clean sturdy spoon. Stir in an easy, steady manner. Do not beat or use an electric mixer. Scrape sides and all parts of pan. Fudge thickens and holds its own shape in 4 to 10 minutes. *TO KNOW IF FUDGE HAS THICKENED ENOUGH:* Stop stirring. Count off 5 seconds. If fudge is still spreading out, resume stirring. Repeat until fudge holds its shape. *WITHOUT A MOMENT'S DELAY, SCOOP FUDGE ONTO PLASTIC WRAP, USING THE SPATULA.* Cool. Wrap tightly. Fudge tastes best after it has aged for 12 hours.

Variations

ALMOND CARAMEL CREME FUDGE
Decrease vanilla to ½ teaspoon. Add ½ teaspoon almond extract.

BANANA CARAMEL CREME FUDGE
Substitute 1 teaspoon banana extract for vanilla.

COCONUT CARAMEL CREME FUDGE
Omit vanilla. Add 1 teaspoon coconut extract.

ORANGE CARAMEL CREME FUDGE
Omit vanilla. Add 2 teaspoons orange extract and 1½ teaspoons grated orange rind.

COFFEE CREME FUDGE

MAKES 1 POUND

INGREDIENTS

2 cups (450 g) sugar
1 cup (240 mL) milk
2 tablespoons light corn syrup
1 tablespoon + 1 teaspoon
instant coffee granules
¼ teaspoon salt
2 tablespoons (28 g) butter, cut
into several pieces
1 teaspoon vanilla extract
Optional: ½ cup (60 g) nuts

Good with roasted whole nuts.

Find your finish temperature on page 14.

Set out on countertop stirring pan, 20-inch sheet of plastic wrap, spatula, timer or clock, and paper and pencil.

BEGIN COOKING: Combine sugar, milk, corn syrup, coffee and salt in cooking pan. Place thermometer in pan with bulb ½ inch off the bottom. Leave in place until fudge is done. Turn heat to medium high. On a gas stove, look at flame at eye level. Turn flame to highest point, then back to medium; carefully adjust to medium high. On a large electric burner, medium heat may be appropriate. Stir to mix well.

When your first temperature level is reached, set a timer for 5 minutes (or jot down the time and watch a clock). Stir frequently or constantly if your pan is thin. Scrape sides and bottom of pan as you stir. After 5 minutes, thermometer should reach your second temperature level. If it reads higher, slightly lower heat. If it reads lower, slightly raise heat.

Immediately set timer for 5 minutes again. After this 5 minutes, the thermometer should reach your third temperature level. If it reads higher or lower, adjust heat as before.

Stir constantly now and watch thermometer closely. In about 5 minutes, when thermometer reaches your EXACT finish temperature, IMMEDIATELY REMOVE FROM HEAT. Remove thermometer.

POUR INTO STIRRING PAN: Do not scrape cooking pan. Let fudge cool at room temperature for 5 minutes. Add butter, vanilla extract and nuts.

BEGIN STIRRING: Use a clean sturdy spoon. Stir in an easy, steady manner. Do not beat or use an electric mixer. Scrape sides and all parts of pan. Fudge thickens and holds its own shape in 4 to 10 minutes. TO KNOW IF FUDGE

HAS THICKENED ENOUGH: Stop stirring. Count off 5 seconds. If fudge is still spreading out, resume stirring. Repeat until fudge holds its shape. WITHOUT A MOMENT'S DELAY, SCOOP FUDGE ONTO PLASTIC WRAP, USING THE SPATULA. Cool. Wrap tightly. Fudge tastes best after it has aged for 12 hours.

Variation

KAHLÚA CREME FUDGE
Add ¼ cup (60 mL) Kahlúa liqueur* to the cooking pan. Omit vanilla.

---

*Alcohol may cause the cooking syrup to foam to the top of the pan. Lower heat until foaming subsides.

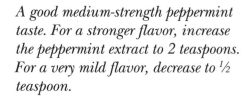

PEPPERMINT CREME FUDGE

MAKES 1 POUND

INGREDIENTS

2 cups (450 g) sugar
1 cup (240 mL) milk
2 tablespoons light corn syrup
¼ teaspoon salt
2 tablespoons (28 g) butter, cut
into several pieces
1 teaspoon peppermint extract

A good medium-strength peppermint taste. For a stronger flavor, increase the peppermint extract to 2 teaspoons. For a very mild flavor, decrease to ½ teaspoon.

Find your finish temperature on page 14.

Set out on countertop stirring pan, 20-inch sheet of plastic wrap, spatula, timer or clock, and paper and pencil.

BEGIN COOKING: Combine sugar, milk, corn syrup and salt in cooking pan. Place thermometer in pan with bulb ½ inch off the bottom. Leave in place until fudge is done. Turn heat to medium high. On a gas stove, look at flame at eye level. Turn flame to highest point, then back to medium; carefully adjust to medium high. On a large electric burner, medium heat may be appropriate. Stir to mix well.

When your first temperature level is reached, set a timer for 5 minutes (or jot down the time and watch a clock). Stir frequently or constantly if your pan is thin. Scrape sides and bottom

Opposite: Coconut Creme Fudge (p. 52)

of pan as you stir. After 5 minutes, thermometer should reach your second temperature level. If it reads higher, slightly lower heat. If it reads lower, slightly raise heat.

Immediately set timer for 5 minutes again. After this 5 minutes, the thermometer should reach your third temperature level. If it reads higher or lower, adjust heat as before.

Stir constantly now and watch thermometer closely. In about 5 minutes, when thermometer reaches your EXACT finish temperature, IMMEDIATELY REMOVE FROM HEAT. Remove thermometer.

POUR INTO STIRRING PAN: Do not scrape cooking pan. Let fudge cool at room temperature for 5 minutes. Add butter and peppermint extract.

BEGIN STIRRING: Use a clean sturdy spoon. Stir in an easy, steady manner. Do not beat or use an electric mixer. Scrape sides and all parts of pan. Fudge thickens and holds its own shape in 4 to 10 minutes. TO KNOW IF FUDGE HAS THICKENED ENOUGH: Stop stirring. Count off 5 seconds. If fudge is still spreading out, resume stirring. Repeat until fudge holds its shape. WITHOUT A MOMENT'S DELAY, SCOOP FUDGE ONTO PLASTIC WRAP, USING THE SPATULA. Cool. Wrap tightly. Fudge tastes best after it has aged for 12 hours.

Variation

CRÈME DE MENTHE CREME FUDGE
This is a bright minty green, perfect for Christmas if you use green crème de menthe; use clear crème de menthe for a pure white fudge.

Add ¼ cup (60 mL) crème de menthe* to the cooking pan. Reduce peppermint to ½ teaspoon.

---

*Alcohol may cause the cooking syrup to foam to the top of the pan. Lower heat until foaming subsides.

Opposite: Crème de Menthe Creme Fudge

GINGER CREME FUDGE

MAKES 1 POUND

INGREDIENTS

2 cups (450 g) sugar
1 cup (240 mL) milk
2 tablespoons light corn syrup
¼ teaspoon salt
2 tablespoons (28 g) butter, cut into
several pieces
1 teaspoon ginger extract

Find your finish temperature on page 14.

Set out on countertop stirring pan, 20-inch sheet of plastic wrap, spatula, timer or clock, and paper and pencil.

BEGIN COOKING: Combine sugar, milk, corn syrup and salt in cooking pan. Place thermometer in pan with bulb ½ inch off the bottom. Leave in place until fudge is done. Turn heat to medium high. On a gas stove, look at flame at eye level. Turn flame to highest point, then back to medium; carefully adjust to medium high. On a large electric burner, medium heat may be appropriate. Stir to mix well.

When your first temperature level is reached, set a timer for 5 minutes (or jot down the time and watch a clock). Stir frequently or constantly if your pan is thin. Scrape sides and bottom of pan as you stir. After 5 minutes, thermometer should reach your second temperature level. If it reads higher, slightly lower heat. If it reads lower, slightly raise heat.

Immediately set timer for 5 minutes again. After this 5 minutes, the thermometer should reach your third temperature level. If it reads higher or lower, adjust heat as before.

Stir constantly now and watch thermometer closely. In about 5 minutes, when thermometer reaches your EXACT finish temperature, IMMEDIATELY REMOVE FROM HEAT. Remove thermometer.

POUR INTO STIRRING PAN: Do not scrape cooking pan. Let fudge cool at room temperature for 5 minutes. Add butter and ginger extract.

BEGIN STIRRING: Use a clean sturdy spoon. Stir in an easy, steady manner. Do not beat or use an electric mixer. Scrape sides and all parts of pan. Fudge thickens and holds its own shape in 4 to 10 minutes. TO KNOW IF FUDGE HAS THICKENED ENOUGH: Stop stirring. Count off 5 seconds. If fudge is still spreading out, resume stirring. Repeat until fudge holds its

shape. WITHOUT A MOMENT'S DELAY, SCOOP FUDGE ONTO PLASTIC WRAP, USING THE SPATULA. Cool. Wrap tightly. Fudge tastes best after it has aged for 12 hours.

Variation

LEMON GINGER CREME FUDGE
Add ½ teaspoon lemon extract.

HONEY CREME FUDGE

MAKES 1 POUND

INGREDIENTS

1¾ cups (400 g) sugar
1 cup (240 mL) milk
2 tablespoons honey
⅛ teaspoon baking soda
2 tablespoons (28 g) butter, cut
into several pieces
½ teaspoon vanilla extract
Optional: ½ cup (60 g) nuts

As it cooks, this fudge slowly turns golden brown and becomes very thick and viscous. Stir constantly to avoid burning. Be prepared to stir a very heavy mass of fudge; use a good sturdy wooden spoon.

Add 8°F (5° C) to your finish temperature on page 14.

Set out on countertop stirring pan, 20-inch sheet of plastic wrap, spatula, timer or clock, and paper and pencil.

BEGIN COOKING: Combine sugar, milk, honey, and baking soda in cooking pan. Place thermometer in pan with bulb ½ inch off the bottom. Leave in place until fudge is done. Turn heat to medium high. On a gas stove, look at flame at eye level. Turn flame to highest point, then back to medium; carefully adjust to medium high. On a large electric burner, medium heat may be appropriate. Stir to mix well.*

---

*Baking soda may cause the cooking syrup to foam to the top of the pan. Lower heat until foaming subsides.

When your first temperature level is reached, set a timer for 5 minutes (or jot down the time and watch a clock). Stir frequently or constantly if your pan is thin. Scrape sides and bottom of pan as you stir. After 5 minutes, thermometer should reach your second temperature level. If it reads higher, slightly lower heat. If it reads lower, slightly raise heat.

Immediately set timer for 5 minutes again. After this 5 minutes, the thermometer should reach your third temperature level. If it reads higher or lower, adjust heat as before.

Stir constantly now and watch thermometer closely. In about 9 minutes, when thermometer reaches your EXACT finish temperature, IMMEDIATELY REMOVE FROM HEAT. Remove thermometer.

POUR INTO STIRRING PAN: Do not scrape cooking pan. Let fudge cool at room temperature for 5 minutes. Add butter, extracts and nuts.

BEGIN STIRRING: Use a clean sturdy spoon. Stir in an easy, steady manner. Do not beat or use an electric mixer. Scrape sides and all parts of pan. Fudge thickens and holds its own shape in 4 to 10 minutes. TO KNOW IF FUDGE HAS THICKENED ENOUGH: Stop stirring. Count off 5 seconds. If fudge is still spreading out, resume stirring. Repeat until fudge holds its shape. WITHOUT A MOMENT'S DELAY, SCOOP FUDGE ONTO PLASTIC WRAP, USING THE SPATULA. Cool. Wrap tightly. Fudge tastes best after it has aged for 12 hours.

Variations

HONEY ALMOND CREME FUDGE
Reduce vanilla extract to ½ teaspoon. Add ½ teaspoon almond extract.

Optional: ½ cup (60 g) roasted, slivered almonds.

HONEY BANANA CREME FUDGE
Substitute 1 teaspoon banana extract for vanilla.

HONEY BUTTER CREME FUDGE

Add 4 tablespoons (60 g) butter to cooking pan.

HONEY COCONUT CREME FUDGE

Substitute 1 teaspoon coconut extract for vanilla.

Optional: ½ cup (60 g) dried coconut.

NURSE MERRILL'S HONEY LEMON CREME FUDGE

Merrill Reynolds is a young, thoroughly modern nurse who tells of a home cough remedy that her mother gave her as a child—a lovely concoction of sugar, lemon and honey, which happens to contain the very same ingredients that make up this fudge. This is good—maybe it's even good for you!

Substitute 1 teaspoon lemon extract for vanilla.

HONEY RUM CREME FUDGE

Add ¼ cup (60 g) rum,[*] dark preferred, to the cooking pan. Omit vanilla.

---

[*]Alcohol may cause the cooking syrup to foam to the top of the pan. Lower heat until foaming subsides.

Find your finish temperature on page 14.

Set out on countertop stirring pan, 20-inch sheet of plastic wrap, spatula, timer or clock, and paper and pencil.

BEGIN COOKING: Combine sugar, water, milk, corn syrup and salt in cooking pan. Place thermometer in pan with bulb ½ inch off the bottom. Leave in place until fudge is done. Turn heat to medium high. On a gas stove, look at flame at eye level. Turn flame to highest point, then back to medium; carefully adjust to medium high. On a large electric burner, medium heat may be appropriate. Stir to mix well.

When your first temperature level is reached, set a timer for 5 minutes (or jot down the time and watch a clock). Stir frequently or constantly if your pan is thin. Scrape sides and bottom of pan as you stir. After 5 minutes, thermometer should reach your second temperature level. If it reads higher,

BANANA CREME FUDGE

MAKES 1 POUND

INGREDIENTS

2 cups (450 g) sugar
¼ cup (60 mL) water
¾ cup (180 mL) canned evaporated milk
2 tablespoons light corn syrup
¼ teaspoon salt
2 tablespoons (28 g) butter, cut into several pieces
1 teaspoon vanilla extract
1 teaspoon banana extract
Optional: ½ cup (60 g) nuts

slightly lower heat. If it reads lower, slightly raise heat.

Immediately set timer for 5 minutes again. After this 5 minutes, the thermometer should reach your third temperature level. If it reads higher or lower, adjust heat as before.

Stir constantly now and watch thermometer closely. In about 5 minutes, when thermometer reaches your EXACT finish temperature, IMMEDIATELY REMOVE FROM HEAT. Remove thermometer.

POUR INTO STIRRING PAN: Do not scrape cooking pan. Let fudge cool at room temperature for 5 minutes. Add butter, extracts and nuts.

BEGIN STIRRING: Use a clean sturdy spoon. Stir in an easy, steady manner. Do not beat or use an electric mixer. Scrape sides and all parts of pan. Fudge thickens and holds its own shape in 4 to 10 minutes. TO KNOW IF FUDGE HAS THICKENED ENOUGH:

Stop stirring. Count off 5 seconds. If fudge is still spreading out, resume stirring. Repeat until fudge holds its shape. WITHOUT A MOMENT'S DELAY, SCOOP FUDGE ONTO PLASTIC WRAP, USING THE SPATULA. Cool. Wrap tightly. Fudge tastes best after it has aged for 12 hours.

Variation

BANANA RUM CREME FUDGE
Add ¼ cup (60 mL) rum,* dark preferred, to the cooking pan. Omit vanilla.

Optional: ½ cup (60 g) nuts or dried coconut.

---

*Alcohol may cause the cooking syrup to foam to the top of the pan. Lower heat until foaming subsides.

Opposite: Jalapeño Creme Fudge (p. 86)

Find your finish temperature on page 14.

Set out on countertop stirring pan, 20-inch sheet of plastic wrap, spatula, timer or clock, and paper and pencil.

BEGIN COOKING: Combine sugar, milk, corn syrup and salt in cooking pan. Place thermometer in pan with bulb ½ inch off the bottom. Leave in place until fudge is done. Turn heat to medium high. On a gas stove, look at flame at eye level. Turn flame to highest point, then back to medium; carefully adjust to medium high. On a large electric burner, medium heat may be appropriate. Stir to mix well.

When your first temperature level is reached, set a timer for 5 minutes (or jot down the time and watch a clock). Stir frequently or constantly if your pan is thin. Scrape sides and bottom of pan as you stir. After 5 minutes, thermometer should reach your second temperature level. If it reads higher, slightly lower heat. If it reads lower, slightly raise heat.

CHERRY CREME FUDGE

MAKES 1 POUND

INGREDIENTS

2 cups (450 g) sugar
1 cup (240 mL) milk
2 tablespoons light corn syrup
¼ teaspoon salt
2 tablespoons (28 g) butter, cut into several pieces
1¾ teaspoons cherry extract
¼ teaspoon almond extract
Optional: ½ cup (60 g) nuts and/or ½ cup (60 g) minced, dried, pitted sour cherries

Opposite: Cherry Creme Fudge

Immediately set timer for 5 minutes again. After this 5 minutes, the thermometer should reach your third temperature level. If it reads higher or lower, adjust heat as before.

Stir constantly now and watch thermometer closely. In about 5 minutes, when thermometer reaches your EXACT finish temperature, IMMEDIATELY REMOVE FROM HEAT. Remove thermometer.

POUR INTO STIRRING PAN: Do not scrape cooking pan. Let fudge cool at room temperature for 5 minutes. Add butter, extracts and nuts or fruit.

BEGIN STIRRING: Use a clean sturdy spoon. Stir in an easy, steady manner. Do not beat or use an electric mixer. Scrape sides and all parts of pan. Fudge thickens and holds its own shape in 4 to 10 minutes. TO KNOW IF FUDGE HAS THICKENED ENOUGH: Stop stirring. Count off 5 seconds. If fudge is still spreading out, resume stirring. Repeat until fudge holds its

shape. WITHOUT A MOMENT'S DELAY, SCOOP FUDGE ONTO PLASTIC WRAP, USING THE SPATULA. Cool. Wrap tightly. Fudge tastes best after it has aged for 12 hours.

Variation

SOUR CHERRY CREME FUDGE
Omit milk. Add ½ cup (114 g) commercial sour cream mixed with ½ cup (120 mL) water to the cooking pan.

Pure lemon flavor.

Find your finish temperature on page 14.

Set out on countertop stirring pan, 20-inch sheet of plastic wrap, spatula, timer or clock, and paper and pencil.

BEGIN COOKING: Combine sugar, milk, corn syrup and salt in cooking pan. Place thermometer in pan with bulb ½ inch off the bottom. Leave in place until fudge is done. Turn heat to medium high. On a gas stove, look at flame at eye level. Turn flame to highest point, then back to medium; carefully adjust to medium high. On a large electric burner, medium heat may be appropriate. Stir to mix well.

When your first temperature level is reached, set a timer for 5 minutes (or jot down the time and watch a clock). Stir frequently or constantly if your pan is thin. Scrape sides and bottom of pan as you stir. After 5 minutes, thermometer should reach your second temperature level. If it reads higher,

LEMON CREME FUDGE

MAKES 1 POUND

INGREDIENTS

2 cups (450 g) sugar
1 cup (240 mL) milk
2 tablespoons light corn syrup
¼ teaspoon salt
2 tablespoons (28 g) butter, cut
into several pieces
1 teaspoon lemon extract
2 teaspoons grated lemon rind
Optional: ½ cup (60 g) nuts

slightly lower heat. If it reads lower, slightly raise heat.

Immediately set timer for 5 minutes again. After this 5 minutes, the thermometer should reach your third temperature level. If it reads higher or lower, adjust heat as before.

Stir constantly now and watch thermometer closely. In about 5 minutes, when thermometer reaches your EXACT finish temperature, IMMEDIATELY REMOVE FROM HEAT. Remove thermometer.

POUR INTO STIRRING PAN: Do not scrape cooking pan. Let fudge cool at room temperature for 5 minutes. Add butter, lemon extract, lemon rind and nuts.

BEGIN STIRRING: Use a clean sturdy spoon. Stir in an easy, steady manner. Do not beat or use an electric mixer. Scrape sides and all parts of pan. Fudge thickens and holds its own shape in 4 to 10 minutes. TO KNOW IF FUDGE

HAS THICKENED ENOUGH: Stop stirring. Count off 5 seconds. If fudge is still spreading out, resume stirring. Repeat until fudge holds its shape. WITHOUT A MOMENT'S DELAY, SCOOP FUDGE ONTO PLASTIC WRAP, USING THE SPATULA. Cool. Wrap tightly. Fudge tastes best after it has aged for 12 hours.

Variations

SOUR LEMON CREME FUDGE
A little tart, with slightly lingering sour taste.

Omit milk. Add ½ cup (114 g) commercial sour cream mixed with ½ cup (120 mL) water to the cooking pan. Increase lemon extract to 1½ teaspoons.

LEMON ORANGE CREME FUDGE
Reduce lemon extract to ½ teaspoon and lemon rind to 1 teaspoon. Add ½ teaspoon orange extract

and 1½ teaspoons grated orange rind.

LIME CREME FUDGE
Substitute 1 teaspoon lime extract and 1 teaspoon grated lime rind for lemon extract and lemon rind.

APRICOT CREME FUDGE
Omit lemon rind. Increase lemon extract to 1½ teaspoons. Add ½ teaspoon orange extract and 12 minced dried apricots.

FRUITY CREME FUDGE
Chock full of fruits and nuts. Decrease lemon rind to 1 teaspoon and nuts to ¼ cup (30 g). Add ½ teaspoon grated lime rind, 6 minced dried apricots and ¼ cup (30 g) dried coconut.

ORANGE CREME FUDGE

MAKES 1 POUND

INGREDIENTS

2 cups (450 g) sugar
1 cup (240 mL) milk
2 tablespoons light corn syrup
¼ teaspoon salt
2 tablespoons (28 g) butter, cut
into several pieces
1 teaspoon orange extract
1 tablespoon grated orange rind
Optional: ½ cup (60 g) nuts

Find your finish temperature on page 14.

Set out on countertop stirring pan, 20-inch sheet of plastic wrap, spatula, timer or clock, and paper and pencil.

Combine sugar, milk, corn syrup and salt in cooking pan. Place thermometer in pan with bulb ½ inch off the bottom. Leave in place until fudge is done. Turn heat to medium high. On a gas stove, look at flame at eye level. Turn flame to highest point, then back to medium; carefully adjust to medium high. On a large electric burner, medium heat may be appropriate. Stir to mix well.

When your first temperature level is reached, set a timer for 5 minutes (or jot down the time and watch a clock). Stir frequently or constantly if your pan is thin. Scrape sides and bottom of pan as you stir. After 5 minutes, thermometer should reach your second temperature level. If it reads higher, slightly lower heat. If it reads lower, slightly raise heat.

Immediately set timer for 5 minutes again. After this 5 minutes, the thermometer should reach your third temperature level. If it reads higher or lower, adjust heat as before.

Stir constantly now and watch thermometer closely. In about 5 minutes, when thermometer reaches your EXACT finish temperature, IMMEDIATELY REMOVE FROM HEAT. Remove thermometer.

POUR INTO STIRRING PAN: Do not scrape cooking pan. Let fudge cool at room temperature for 5 minutes. Add butter, orange extract, orange rind and nuts.

BEGIN STIRRING: Use a clean sturdy spoon. Stir in an easy, steady manner. Do not beat or use an electric mixer. Scrape sides and all parts of pan. Fudge thickens and holds its own shape in 4 to 10 minutes. TO KNOW IF FUDGE HAS THICKENED ENOUGH: Stop stirring. Count off 5 seconds. If fudge is still spreading out, resume stirring. Repeat until fudge holds its

shape. WITHOUT A MOMENT'S DELAY, SCOOP FUDGE ONTO PLASTIC WRAP, USING THE SPATULA. Cool. Wrap tightly. Fudge tastes best after it has aged for 12 hours.

Variation

SOUR ORANGE CREME FUDGE
Omit milk. Add ½ cup (114 g) commercial sour cream mixed with ½ cup (120 mL) water to the cooking pan. Omit orange rind.

PINEAPPLE CREME FUDGE

MAKES 1 POUND

INGREDIENTS

2 cups (450 g) sugar
1 cup (240 mL) milk
2 tablespoons light corn syrup
¼ teaspoon salt
2 tablespoons (28 g) butter, cut
into several pieces
2 teaspoons pineapple extract
Optional: ½ cup (60 g) nuts or
dried coconut

Find your finish temperature on page 14.

Set out on countertop stirring pan, 20-inch sheet of plastic wrap, spatula, timer or clock, and paper and pencil.

BEGIN COOKING: Combine sugar, milk, corn syrup and salt in cooking pan. Place thermometer in pan with bulb ½ inch off the bottom. Leave in place until fudge is done. Turn heat to medium high. On a gas stove, look at flame at eye level. Turn flame to highest point, then back to medium; carefully adjust to medium high. On a large electric burner, medium heat may be appropriate. Stir to mix well.

When your first temperature level is reached, set a timer for 5 minutes (or jot down the time and watch a clock). Stir frequently or constantly if your pan is thin. Scrape sides and bottom of pan as you stir. After 5 minutes, thermometer should reach your second temperature level. If it reads higher, slightly lower heat. If it reads lower, slightly raise heat.

Immediately set timer for 5 minutes again. After this 5 minutes, the thermometer should reach your third temperature level. If it reads higher or lower, adjust heat as before.

Stir constantly now and watch thermometer closely. In about 5 minutes, when thermometer reaches your EXACT finish temperature, IMMEDIATELY REMOVE FROM HEAT. Remove thermometer.

POUR INTO STIRRING PAN: Do not scrape cooking pan. Let fudge cool at room temperature for 5 minutes. Add butter, pineapple extract and nuts or coconut.

BEGIN STIRRING: Use a clean sturdy spoon. Stir in an easy, steady manner. Do not beat or use an electric mixer. Scrape sides and all parts of pan. Fudge thickens and holds its own shape in 4 to 10 minutes. TO KNOW IF FUDGE HAS THICKENED ENOUGH: Stop stirring. Count off 5 seconds. If fudge is still spreading out, resume stirring. Repeat until fudge holds its

shape. WITHOUT A MOMENT'S DELAY, SCOOP FUDGE ONTO PLASTIC WRAP, USING THE SPATULA. Cool. Wrap tightly. Fudge tastes best after it has aged for 12 hours.

Variation

PINEAPPLE RUM CREME FUDGE
Add ¼ cup (60 mL) rum,* dark preferred, to the cooking pan.

**Alcohol may cause the cooking syrup to foam to the top of the pan. Lower heat until foaming subsides.*

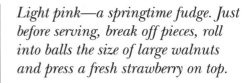

STRAWBERRY CREME FUDGE

MAKES 1 POUND

INGREDIENTS

2 cups (450 g) sugar
1 cup (240 mL) milk
2 tablespoons light corn syrup
¼ teaspoon salt
2 tablespoons (28 g) butter, cut
into several pieces
2 teaspoons strawberry extract
Optional: ½ (60 g) cup dried
coconut

Light pink—a springtime fudge. Just before serving, break off pieces, roll into balls the size of large walnuts and press a fresh strawberry on top.

Find your finish temperature on page 14.

Set out on countertop stirring pan, 20-inch sheet of plastic wrap, spatula, timer or clock, and paper and pencil.

BEGIN COOKING: Combine sugar, milk, corn syrup and salt in cooking pan. Place thermometer in pan with bulb ½ inch off the bottom. Leave in place until fudge is done. Turn heat to medium high. On a gas stove, look at flame at eye level. Turn flame to highest point, then back to medium; carefully adjust to medium high. On a large electric burner, medium heat may be appropriate. Stir to mix well.

When your first temperature level is reached, set a timer for 5 minutes (or jot down the time and watch a clock). Stir frequently or constantly if your pan is thin. Scrape sides and bottom of pan as you stir. After 5 minutes, thermometer should reach your second temperature level. If it reads higher, slightly lower heat. If it reads lower, slightly raise heat.

Immediately set timer for 5 minutes again. After this 5 minutes, the thermometer should reach your third temperature level. If it reads higher or lower, adjust heat as before.

Stir constantly now and watch thermometer closely. In about 5 minutes, when thermometer reaches your EXACT finish temperature, IMMEDIATELY REMOVE FROM HEAT. Remove thermometer.

POUR INTO STIRRING PAN: Do not scrape cooking pan. Let fudge cool at room temperature for 5 minutes. Add butter, strawberry extract and coconut.

BEGIN STIRRING: Use a clean sturdy spoon. Stir in an easy, steady manner. Do not beat or use an electric mixer. Scrape sides and all parts of pan. Fudge thickens and holds its own shape in 4 to 10 minutes. TO KNOW IF FUDGE HAS THICKENED ENOUGH: Stop stirring. Count off 5 seconds. If fudge is still spreading out, resume stirring. Repeat until fudge holds its shape. WITHOUT A MOMENT'S DELAY, SCOOP FUDGE ONTO PLASTIC WRAP, USING THE SPATULA. Cool. Wrap tightly. Fudge tastes best after it has aged for 12 hours.

TROPICAL MADNESS CREME FUDGE

MAKES 1 POUND

INGREDIENTS

2 cups (450 g) sugar
1 cup (240 mL) milk
2 tablespoons light corn syrup
¼ teaspoon salt
2 tablespoons (28 g) butter, cut
into several pieces
½ teaspoon banana extract
½ teaspoon coconut extract
½ teaspoon pineapple extract
½ teaspoon strawberry extract
Optional: ½ cup (60 g) nuts or
dried coconut

Wild combinations of fruit flavors! Try making up your own mixture of extracts, not to exceed 2 teaspoons.

Find your finish temperature on page 14.

Set out on countertop stirring pan, 20-inch sheet of plastic wrap, spatula, timer or clock, and paper and pencil.

Combine sugar, milk, corn syrup and salt in cooking pan. Place thermometer in pan with bulb ½ inch off the bottom. Leave in place until fudge is done. Turn heat to medium high. On a gas stove, look at flame at eye level. Turn flame to highest point, then back to medium; carefully adjust to medium high. On a large electric burner, medium heat may be appropriate. Stir to mix well.

When your first temperature level is reached, set a timer for 5 minutes (or jot down the time and watch a clock). Stir frequently or constantly if your pan is thin. Scrape sides and bottom of pan as you stir. After 5 minutes,

thermometer should reach your second temperature level. If it reads higher, slightly lower heat. If it reads lower, slightly raise heat.

Immediately set timer for 5 minutes again. After this 5 minutes, the thermometer should reach your third temperature level. If it reads higher or lower, adjust heat as before.

Stir constantly now and watch thermometer closely. In about 5 minutes, when thermometer reaches your EXACT finish temperature, IM-MEDIATELY REMOVE FROM HEAT. Remove thermometer.

POUR INTO STIRRING PAN: Do not scrape cooking pan. Let fudge cool at room temperature for 5 minutes. Add butter, extracts and nuts or coconut.

BEGIN STIRRING: Use a clean sturdy spoon. Stir in an easy, steady manner. Do not beat or use an electric mixer. Scrape sides and all parts of pan. Fudge thickens and holds its own shape in 4 to 10 minutes. TO KNOW IF FUDGE HAS THICKENED ENOUGH: Stop stirring. Count off 5 seconds. If fudge is still spreading out, resume stirring. Repeat until fudge holds its shape. WITHOUT A MOMENT'S DELAY, SCOOP FUDGE ONTO PLASTIC WRAP, USING THE SPATULA. Cool. Wrap tightly. Fudge tastes best after it has aged for 12 hours.

Variation

KIDS' FUDGE
Tastes like bubble gum! For the above combination of extracts, substitute ¾ teaspoon strawberry extract, ½ teaspoon pineapple extract and ¼ teaspoon each coconut, banana and lemon extracts.

Optional: ½ cup (60 g) nuts or dried coconut.

JALAPEÑO CREME FUDGE

MAKES 1 POUND

INGREDIENTS

2 cups (450 g) sugar
1 cup (240 mL) milk
2 tablespoons light corn syrup
¼ teaspoon salt
2 tablespoons (28 g) butter
1 tablespoon canned diced
jalapeño chilies,
thoroughly rinsed and patted dry

Hot sweet fun! Jalapeño chilies (also called peppers) are very hot by themselves but the sugar tames them some. Freeze leftover chilies for other uses.

Find your finish temperature on page 14.

Set out on countertop stirring pan, 20-inch sheet of plastic wrap, spatula, timer or clock, and paper and pencil.

BEGIN COOKING: Combine sugar, milk, corn syrup and salt in cooking pan. Place thermometer in pan with bulb ½ inch off the bottom. Leave in place until fudge is done. Turn heat to medium high. On a gas stove, look at flame at eye level. Turn flame to highest point, then back to medium; carefully adjust to medium high. On a large electric burner, medium heat may be appropriate. Stir to mix well.

When your first temperature level is reached, set a timer for 5 minutes (or jot down the time and watch a clock). Stir frequently or constantly if your pan is thin. Scrape sides and bottom of pan as you stir. After 5 minutes, thermometer should reach your second temperature level. If it reads higher, slightly lower heat. If it reads lower, slightly raise heat.

Immediately set timer for 5 minutes again. After this 5 minutes, the thermometer should reach your third temperature level. If it reads higher or lower, adjust heat as before.

Stir constantly now and watch thermometer closely. In about 5 minutes, when thermometer reaches your EXACT finish temperature, IMMEDIATELY REMOVE FROM HEAT. Remove thermometer.

POUR INTO STIRRING PAN: Do not scrape cooking pan. Let fudge cool at room temperature for 5 minutes. Add butter and jalapeños.

BEGIN STIRRING: Use a clean sturdy spoon. Stir in an easy, steady manner. Do not beat or use an electric mixer. Scrape sides and all parts of pan. Fudge thickens and holds its own shape in 4 to 10

minutes. TO KNOW IF FUDGE HAS THICKENED ENOUGH: Stop stirring. Count off 5 seconds. If fudge is still spreading out, resume stirring. Repeat until fudge holds its shape. WITHOUT A MOMENT'S DELAY, SCOOP FUDGE ONTO PLASTIC WRAP, USING THE SPATULA. Cool. Wrap tightly. Fudge tastes best after it has aged for 12 hours.

Opposite: Chocolate Burnt Almond Fudge (p. 21)
Overleaf: Fudge failures. Top: hard, caramel-like,
right: dry, crumbly; bottom: sugary;
left: syrupy.

SUCCESS FROM FAILURE

It is puzzling to most people why fudges occasionally fail. But it is surprising to learn that almost all failures can be corrected.

FAILURE	CAUSE	REMEDY
SYRUPY FUDGE	Finish temperature incorrect	Recheck your finish temperature. Recook fudge.
	Not stirred long enough in stirring pan	Recook fudge.
	Cooked too long	Heat fudge.
	Too much syrup used*	None
SUGARY FUDGE	Not enough syrup used	
	Fudge cooled in cooking pan	
	Fudge stirred in stirring pan with syrup-coated spoon	Recook fudge.
	Nuts or fruit added after stirring started	
	Sugared nuts or fruit used	

*Fudges containing too much syrup due to inaccurate measuring cannot be restored. Thin with milk and serve warm as a sauce over cake or ice cream.

FAILURE	CAUSE	REMEDY
DRY, CRUMBLY FUDGE	Cooked too long Was not scooped out of stirring pan fast enough Left unwrapped	Knead fudge.
HARD, CARAMEL-LIKE FUDGE	Finish temperature incorrect	Recheck your finish temperature. Recook fudge.

TO RECOOK FUDGE Return fudge to the clean cooking pan with ½ cup (120 mL) milk. Place thermometer in pan and cook over medium high heat until your finish temperature is reached, stirring constantly. Pour into stirring pan. Let cool for 5 minutes. Stir until fudge thickens, as before. Add fresh extracts if desired. Recooked fudge may be a little dry but kneading will soften it.

TO HEAT FUDGE Set stirring pan over low heat on the stove for about 10 seconds. Remove from heat and stir for several minutes. Repeat if fudge does not thicken.

TO KNEAD FUDGE Dry fudge can be kneaded to an excellent texture. Squeeze pieces like clay in your hands, then press them together. Overkneading softens too much. Kneaded fudge formed into any shape is particularly attractive with nuts pressed onto the surface; salted nuts are delicious.

INDEX

FAVORITE RECIPES

Marilyn Myerly lives in Santa Barbara, California.